M
~
ENTERTAINING

A
FORMAL
DINNER
PARTY

by Martha Stewart

Clarkson N. Potter, Inc./Publishers
DISTRIBUTED BY
CROWN PUBLISHERS, INC., NEW YORK

Martha Stewart would like to thank
Sterling Vineyards of California
for their participation in the production of this video,
and for providing the following wines used in this video:

CABERNET SAUVIGNON
CHARDONNAY
MUMM CHAMPAGNE
SAUVIGNON BLANC

INTRODUCTION

For the past twenty-seven years Andy and I have entertained friends, business associates, and new acquaintances at small sit-down dinner parties. We began with dinners for six or eight friends, served informally in our first apartment. Although we had to do everything ourselves, the menus were elaborate and I often served some spectacular creation I had practiced beforehand.

Now we live in a restored farmhouse in Westport, Connecticut, and we still prefer the sit-down dinner. It can be an extremely informal gathering around the kitchen table or a formal dinner in our Federal-style dining room. If we're in the mood, we wear black tie and evening dresses, but the food is always plated in the kitchen (we don't have serving help) and arranged on china I've been accumulating over the years. Sometimes I serve hors d'oeuvres, and I always make a first course, which might be a colorful soup, a terrine or timbale, or a simple fresh salad. The main course is meat or fish, prepared with a flavorful sauce, and two or three vegetables. I sometimes opt for a cheese and salad course and then finish with a sumptuous dessert.

After dinner, we serve coffee in another room with soft music playing in the background, so the quiet of the house is not evident during pauses in the conversation. Candles are lit and in cold weather fires burn in the fireplaces. We always try to remember that the dinner is for our enjoyment as well as for the guests.

I hope these recipes will inspire you to invite some friends to a sit-down dinner in your home.

MENU

*Cucumber Hearts
with Herb Cheese*

Yeast Blini with Black Caviar

*Heart Toasts with Caviar
and Sour Cream*

*Salmon and Scallop Timbales
with Spinach Sauce*

Roast Loin of Pork

Sautéed Apples

Prunes Macerated in Armagnac

Herb-Vegetable Wild Rice

Puree of Broccoli

*Alternate Entrée:
Stuffed Chicken Breasts*

*Red Currant Ice Cream in
Brandy Snap Cups with
Caramel Sauce and Spun Sugar*

CUCUMBER HEARTS WITH HERB CHEESE

decorative flourish

MAKES 30 TO 40 HORS D'OEUVRES

2 seedless English or Japanese cucumbers, sliced

HERB CHEESE
(MAKES APPROXIMATELY 1¼ CUPS)

- ½ cup heavy cream
- 4 ounces cream cheese, at room temperature
- 1 teaspoon each chopped fresh dill and chervil
- 1 tablespoon chopped fresh parsley
- Dash of cayenne pepper
- 1 teaspoon freshly squeezed lemon juice

Sprigs of fresh dill

To prepare cucumbers, wash each cucumber and cut into slices a little less than ¼ inch thick. Using a heart-shaped cookie or biscuit cutter slightly smaller in diameter than the cucumber slices, cut them into hearts. Place cucumbers on a towel-lined baking sheet, cover with plastic wrap, and refrigerate for up to 3 hours.

To make the herb cheese, whip the heavy cream with an electric mixer until stiff. In a separate bowl, whip the cream cheese with the herbs and other remaining ingredients until light and fluffy. Fold in the whipped cream and refrigerate until ready to use.

No more than 1 hour before serving, remove herb cheese from refrigerator. Using a pastry bag fitted with a decorative tip, pipe the herb cheese onto the cucumber hearts. Garnish each hors d'oeuvre with a sprig of fresh dill.

YEAST BLINI
WITH BLACK CAVIAR

~~/J

MAKES 40 HORS D'OEUVRES

BLINI

- 1 package active dry yeast
- ½ cup warm water
- 1 cup milk
- 1½ cups all-purpose, buckwheat, or whole-wheat flour
- 3 eggs, separated
- ½ teaspoon salt
  Pinch of sugar
- 6 tablespoons (¾ stick) unsalted butter, melted, plus additional for cooking
- 3 or 4 hard-boiled eggs
- 3½ ounces black caviar

To make the blini, first proof the yeast in the warm water for 15 minutes. Combine the yeast mixture, milk, flour, egg yolks, salt, sugar, and melted butter in the bowl of a food processor or blender. Process at high speed for 40 seconds; turn off the machine, scrape down the sides, and blend for a few seconds more. Pour the batter into a large bowl (it will double in volume so the bowl must accommodate this), cover, and set in a warm place for 1½ to 2 hours. (If the dough rises much longer than this, the blini may taste overfermented.)

Mince the hard-boiled egg yolks and egg whites by pushing them, separately, through a strainer. Set aside.

Immediately before cooking the blini, beat the egg whites until stiff and fold them into the batter. Drop the batter by teaspoonfuls onto a hot buttered skillet or griddle, and cook until lightly browned. Turn and briefly cook the other side. Keep the blini on a warm platter until all the batter is used, then place on a serving tray or platter. Spoon caviar, a bit of egg yolk, and egg white on top of the blini. Serve with lemon wedges.

VARIATION Serve with finely minced white onion or sour cream.

HEART TOASTS WITH CAVIAR AND SOUR CREAM

MAKES 24 TO 30 HORS D'OEUVRES

8 thin slices of good white or whole-wheat bread, homemade or store-bought

3½ ounces salmon roe caviar

½ cup sour cream or whipped crème fraîche

Leaves of fine basil or other herbs

Preheat oven to 250°F.

Cut the bread using a heart-shaped cookie or biscuit cutter that will yield 2 to 4 hearts per slice. Place the hearts on a baking sheet and place another baking sheet the same size directly on top of them. Bake until crispy and dry, but not colored, about 10 minutes. Remove from the oven and let cool on a wire rack.

To serve, spoon approximately ½ teaspoon of caviar onto each heart and top with a bit of sour cream or crème fraîche. Garnish with a couple of leaves of fine basil (basilico fino) or other herbs.

SALMON AND SCALLOP TIMBALES

8 timbales, ½ cup each
   Safflower or light vegetable oil
   Sprigs of fresh thyme, chervil, or Italian parsley

SALMON MOUSSE

½ pound fresh salmon, skinned and boned
1 egg white
½ cup heavy cream
   Salt and freshly ground white pepper, to taste
   Freshly ground nutmeg, to taste
   Pinch of cayenne pepper

SCALLOP MOUSSE

¾ pound sea scallops
1 egg white
½ cup heavy cream
   Salt and freshly ground white pepper, to taste
   Freshly ground nutmeg, to taste

8 to 12 fresh spinach leaves, steamed slightly

Preheat oven to 325°F. Put water on to boil in a shallow pan. Brush timbales with the safflower or light vegetable oil. Place a sprig of thyme, chervil, or parsley in the bottom of each timbale.

Place the salmon, egg white, heavy cream, and pinches of salt, pepper, nutmeg, and cayenne pepper in a food processor. Process for several seconds, or just until smooth. Do not overprocess.

Follow the above procedure to prepare the scallop mousse.

Spoon salmon mousse into the timbales until half full. Cover this layer with a steamed spinach leaf. Spoon in the scallop mousse to fill completely. Cover each timbale with a sheet of parchment paper or wax paper.

Place timbales in the shallow pan and pour in boiling water to come halfway up the timbales. Place in oven, reduce heat to 300°F., and bake 30 minutes, or until the internal temperature is between 115°F. and 120°F. Remove timbales from water bath and allow to cool slightly.

Turn out the still warm timbales onto individual plates that have been prepared with Spinach Sauce (recipe follows).

SPINACH SAUCE

MAKES 1 CUP

 1 **pound fresh spinach, well washed**
¼ **cup heavy cream**
 4 **tablespoons (½ stick) unsalted butter**
   Freshly ground nutmeg, to taste
   Salt and freshly ground black pepper, to taste
   Chicken stock to thin, if necessary

Steam spinach a minute or two until wilted. In a food processor, puree spinach with heavy cream and butter. Season to taste with nutmeg, salt, and pepper. Sauce should be about the consistency of heavy cream. If too thick, thin with a little chicken stock. Keep at room temperature.

Spoon onto small plates to make a shallow pool, onto which the timbales will be placed.

ROAST LOIN OF PORK

SERVES 6

1 4- to 5-pound boneless loin of pork (center
    cut), neatly tied, with almost all fat removed
4 teaspoons coarse salt
2 teaspoons freshly ground black pepper
8 bay leaves, crumbled
2 teaspoons fresh thyme
2 teaspoons finely chopped fresh sage
    Approximately ⅛ cup olive oil for browning
    meat
¼ cup Armagnac
    Whole shallots, peeled
    Whole garlic cloves, peeled
    Thyme sprigs
    Sage sprigs

At least one hour before roasting, rub the
loin of pork with salt, pepper, bay leaves,
thyme, and sage. Wrap the pork with this dry
marinade in parchment paper. Let sit at least one
hour at room temperature, or up to 24 hours in
the refrigerator. (Be sure to remove the pork
from the refrigerator one hour before roasting,
however.)

Preheat the oven to 375°F. Line a roasting
pan large enough to hold the pork with alumi-
num foil. Rub excess marinade off the pork.

Heat the olive oil in a heavy skillet and
brown the pork all over for about 6 to 7 minutes. Heat the Armagnac over a low flame. Place
the browned meat in the foil-lined roasting pan
and pour the Armagnac over it. Flame the
brandy with a lighted match and let it burn until

all the alcohol evaporates. Surround the roast with the whole shallots, garlic cloves, thyme sprigs, and sage sprigs. Place the pork in the upper third of the oven and roast for approximately 40 minutes or until the internal temperature registers 160°F. Remove from the oven. Serve immediately.

SAUTÉED APPLES

SERVES 6 TO 8

- 4 tart, firm apples, such as Granny Smith, Cortland, or Rome
- 4 to 6 tablespoons (½ to ¾ stick) unsalted butter
- ¼ cup granulated sugar

Peel the apples. Cut each one into 12 wedges, carefully removing the seeds and core. Melt the butter in a large heavy-bottomed skillet. Add the apple wedges in one layer. Sprinkle the apple wedges with some of the sugar, and sauté over medium heat for a couple of minutes, until they are golden in color. Turn each wedge and sprinkle with more sugar. Turn once more. Sauté until the apples are a light golden brown. Serve immediately.

PRUNES MACERATED IN ARMAGNAC

~///

SERVES 6 TO 8

8 ounces pitted prunes
½ cup Armagnac
  Lemon peel

Macerate the prunes in Armagnac with the lemon peel overnight. Just before serving, heat the prunes in a saucepan.

HERB-VEGETABLE WILD RICE

~///

SERVES 6 TO 8

1½ cups long-grain wild rice
  3 quarts boiling water or stock
  1 cup finely diced carrots
  1 cup finely diced celery
½ cup minced shallots
¼ cup chopped Italian (flat leaf) parsley
  4 tablespoons (½ stick) unsalted butter
  Salt and freshly ground black pepper, to taste

Simmer the wild rice in water or stock until just tender (about 30 to 40 minutes). Drain thoroughly.

Sauté the carrots, celery, and shallots in the butter until just tender. Add chopped parsley. Combine with the cooked rice. Season with salt and pepper. Reheat and serve.

PUREE OF BROCCOLI

SERVES 6

1 large bunch broccoli
¼ cup heavy cream
2 tablespoons butter
Salt and freshly ground black pepper, to taste
Freshly ground nutmeg, or ground cinnamon
to taste

Wash broccoli. Trim off tough stems and divide stalks lengthwise. Steam broccoli until just tender; then plunge immediately into ice water to stop cooking and to preserve the bright green color. When cold, remove from water and drain.

Puree broccoli, heavy cream, butter, salt and pepper, and a pinch of nutmeg or cinnamon in a food processor until not quite smooth. Adjust seasonings to taste. Just before serving, put a little butter in a saucepan, add the puree, and gently reheat, being careful not to scorch the bottom.

NOTE This can be made the day before serving and kept in the refrigerator until time to reheat.

STUFFED CHICKEN BREASTS

~~/♪

SERVES AT LEAST 6

6 whole chicken breasts, halved and boned,
  with the skin left on
5½ ounces chèvre (goat cheese), not too dry
1 tablespoon minced fresh chervil
1 tablespoon minced fresh chives

RED PEPPER JELLY GLAZE

Red pepper jelly
Balsamic vinegar

Place each breast skin side up on a board.
Trim away excess fat.

To make stuffing, combine chèvre, chervil,
and chives and mix well. Loosen skin from one
side of breast and place approximately 2 to 3
tablespoons of stuffing under the skin. Tuck the
skin and meat under the breast, forming an
even, round shape. Put the stuffed breasts in a
foil-lined or buttered Pyrex or metal baking
dish. (The breasts can be baked immediately or
kept covered in the refrigerator up to 24 hours
before baking.)

Fifteen minutes before baking, preheat the
oven to 375°F.

To make the glaze, mix equal parts red pepper jelly and balsamic vinegar. Brush on the fin-
ished breasts. Put the breasts in the oven and
bake until golden brown, about 30 to 35 minutes. Do not overcook or chicken will be dry.
Cool to room temperature if you plan to slice
breasts into small pieces. Arrange on a platter,
spoon leftover glaze over chicken, and garnish,
if desired, with fresh herbs, such as chervil.

N O T E When making this menu with Stuffed Chicken Breasts rather than Roast Loin of Pork, you may prefer to substitute roasted shallots and baby onions for the prunes and sautéed apples.

RED CURRANT ICE CREAM

MAKES ABOUT 1 QUART

1 pint fresh red currants
½ cup half-and-half
½ cup sugar
3 egg yolks
1¼ cups heavy cream
Few drops kirsch and vanilla extract

Strip the currants from their stems. Put them in a stainless-steel saucepan with a few teaspoons of water. Cook 5 to 10 minutes, until tender, then puree in a food mill or processor. Push through a strainer.

In a saucepan over low heat, warm the half-and-half with the sugar until the sugar dissolves. In a small bowl, whisk the egg yolks until just mixed. Add the warm half-and-half, stirring constantly. Return the mixture to the saucepan and cook over low heat. Continue stirring until a custard is formed that coats the spoon. Strain into a bowl and stir in the heavy cream and 6 tablespoons of the currant puree. Add a few drops of kirsch and vanilla to taste. You may wish to add a little more puree to achieve a darker color. Chill thoroughly. Freeze according to the instructions that accompanied your ice-cream maker.

BRANDY SNAP CUPS

MAKES 10 CUPS

8 tablespoons (1 stick) butter
½ cup firmly packed brown sugar
⅓ cup molasses (use dark molasses for darker cups)
¼ teaspoon ground ginger
½ teaspoon ground cinnamon
1 teaspoon grated orange rind
¼ cup flour
2 tablespoons Cognac

Preheat the oven to 325°F.

Have ready three buttered glass ramekins or custard cups measuring about 4½ inches in diameter and 2 inches deep.

Combine the butter, brown sugar, molasses, ginger, cinnamon, and orange rind in a saucepan and bring to a boil. Remove from heat and stir in the flour. Add the Cognac and stir until smooth.

Drop the mixture, 1 tablespoon at a time, onto parchment-covered baking sheets. Space the drops at wide intervals; they spread considerably as they bake. Prepare only three snaps at a time because they harden fast once removed from the oven and may become difficult to shape.

Put the baking sheet in the oven and bake 10 to 12 minutes. Remove from the oven and let cool for a minute or so. Then, one snap at a time, run a thin spatula all around the perimeter to loosen the bottom completely. (If the snaps become hard before removing from the baking sheet, return the baking sheet briefly to the oven.) Quickly place the snap inside one of the ramekins and press down to mold the cup shape. Let cool. Remove the snaps, now molded into cup shapes, from the ramekins.

Continue baking the snaps until all the mixture is used.

To store: Arrange the cups in one layer in airtight plastic or stainless-steel containers and keep in a cool, dry place. Cups can be made a day in advance if they are stored correctly.

CARAMEL SAUCE

MAKES APPROXIMATELY 2 CUPS

1 cup sugar
¼ cup water
1 cup heavy cream
1 teaspoon vanilla extract

In a heavy saucepan or copper sugar pot, melt the sugar in the water over high heat. Do *not* stir mixture—just swirl the pot. Boil until the sugar becomes the color of maple syrup. Be careful not to burn the sugar. Remove from heat and whisk in the heavy cream. Add vanilla. Let cool.

To store: Keep in a closed container in the refrigerator.

SPUN SUGAR

- 2 **cups granulated sugar**
- ⅔ **cup water**
- 2 **tablespoons light corn syrup**
- ⅛ **teaspoon grated beeswax (optional, but highly recommended as beeswax has a high smoking point and will keep the strands flexible for a long time)**

Before making spun sugar, completely cover the floor near your worktable or countertop with newspaper. Tape additional newspaper to the edge of the counter to protect cabinets. Oil the dowels of a wooden clothes rack, or the handle of a long wooden broomstick. If using a broomstick, tape it to the countertop so that the handle extends beyond the edge.

Place the sugar, water, corn syrup, and beeswax together in a small saucepan (an unlined copper pan is preferred). Bring the mixture to a boil over medium heat. Do *not* stir—just swirl the pan. Increase the heat and boil until the liquid turns pale amber, at 260°F. (hard ball) on a candy thermometer. Remove the saucepan from the heat and set the pan in a bowl of cold water. (This will stabilize the temperature so it does not rise anymore. Above 270°F., spun sugar will look brassy instead of golden.) If the mixture is too hot it will fall in droplets instead of strings and will not spin. The optional wax (which is edible) coats the strands of spun sugar, making them easier to work with.

Standing on a stool so that you are above the clothes rack or the wooden broom handle, hold two forks side by side in one hand, or use a cut-off wire whisk. Dip the whisk into the sugar and vigorously wave it back and forth above the rack or broom handle, allowing the strands to fall in long, thin threads. Waving must be continuous or droplets will form. It is normal to have a few small droplets, which are known as angels' tears.

Wrap the strands around the base and sides of the brandy snap cups; it is best to do this immediately after spinning because the strands tend to become brittle and hard to shape after too long. Do not attempt to make spun sugar in hot and/or humid weather, as it will collapse.

To serve Red Currant Ice Cream in Brandy Snap Cups with Caramel Sauce and Spun Sugar, place a scoop of ice cream in each cup and top with caramel sauce. Garnish ice cream with a sprig of fresh red currants and currant or mint leaves. Wrap strands of spun sugar around the base of each cup, creating a cloudlike effect.

Organization

ONE WEEK IN ADVANCE

shop for all nonperishable foods and other items

order liquor, wine, mixers, nonalcoholic beverages, and ice if needed

order meat from butcher

TWO DAYS IN ADVANCE

iron linens, store so they don't crease

wash plates, glasses, serving dishes, etc., if necessary

buy or order flowers

ONE DAY IN ADVANCE

arrange flowers

set table (if possible)

set up bar, if necessary, except for bar fruits and ice

buy perishable foods

make herb cheese, refrigerate

make heart toasts, store in airtight container

macerate prunes in Armagnac, keep covered at room temperature

stuff chicken breasts, refrigerate

make broccoli puree, refrigerate

make red currant ice cream, keep in freezer

make brandy snap cups, store in airtight containers

make caramel sauce

prepare and marinate pork, refrigerate

set table, if necessary
arrange flowers early in the day, if necessary
make cucumber hearts, decorate with herb cheese
top heart toasts with caviar and sour cream
make blini, top with egg and caviar
make salmon and scallop timbales
make spinach sauce
make sautéed apples
cook pork loin
heat prunes
bake stuffed chicken breasts
heat broccoli puree
make herb-vegetable wild rice
make spun sugar
put ice and bar fruits on bar
arrange hors d'oeuvres on trays

Martha Stewart's
TIPS *for*
Perfect Entertaining

Organization is the key to success in any entertaining endeavor; an orderly plan, well and carefully executed, can assure a successful event.

TIPS FOR EVERY PARTY

Carefully plan the date, time, place, and duration of the party.

Plan a menu that can be executed perfectly by you. Don't be overly ambitious or you will spend most of your time in the kitchen.

If you want a menu that is more complicated than you yourself can cook, hire someone to help, possibly even a professional caterer.

Do all of the shopping beforehand. Write out complete shopping lists and cross off items as you purchase them.

Don't be inflexible when it comes to your menu—if asparagus is unavailable, look for an alternative.

Do as much of the preparation in advance as possible. Go over each recipe so that you can plan an effective cooking schedule. Know which dishes can be prepared ahead and frozen.

Often part or all of a dessert can be made way in advance.

Set the table and make the centerpieces a day in advance if you can, and be sure the linens are ironed.

Overreaching is the worst thing one can do when entertaining—if this menu seems a lot to attempt all at once, make only one or two of the recipes, along with recipes of your own. Add more as you become more proficient.

TIPS FOR A DINNER PARTY

On the day of the dinner, make a work plan and timetable for yourself. Gauge how long each task will take and try to keep to your schedule. For example, it takes time to open wine bottles, so even that must be written into the timetable.

Leave yourself plenty of time to take a walk, shower, and rest, as well as sufficient time to dress or fix makeup.

Delegate some of the chores to others—the bar is a good example. Let someone else attend to the drink-making. Make sure there are plenty of mixers, bar fruits, appropriate beverages, and ice.

Have all the dinner plates ready—for the first course, main course, salad, and dessert. Warm plates for hot foods, chill plates for cold desserts.

To ease the burden of cleanup have a sinkful of warm soapy water for the dirty flatware. Put flatware in the water after each course is cleared. Scrape the dishes with a rubber scraper as they are brought into the kitchen. I never wash up while guests are present— and it is one of my unspoken rules that no guests wash dishes in my house.

Try to be relaxed and cheerful and don't rush things. Even if you experience delays in the kitchen, don't let your guests feel the tension.

Serve everything at a leisurely pace and try to keep up with the conversation around you.

If a several-course meal is to be served, prepare only 3 to 4 hors d'oeuvres (2 or 3 of each per guest). Make them light and not too highly seasoned.

Try to decide exactly how much each guest can consume and order food accordingly. If salmon steaks are to be served, for example, provide 1 per person (order 2 or 3 extra for the men). Count asparagus by the serving—8 or 10 pencil asparagus per person, or 5 or 6 medium. One cup of uncooked rice will serve 4 to 5 as a side dish. A handful of salad is enough for a single serving.

For table decorations, try to use seasonal flowers, foliage, and vegetables; this saves money and encourages ingenuity. If no flowers are blooming, use a group of collectibles—yellowware bowls, antique toys, a cluster of seashells, etc.

Eclecticism is in where table settings are concerned! Don't worry about having only one matching set of dishes—mix and match on tables, and fill in with rented dishes and glassware for larger parties.

A theme often helps when planning an at-home dinner or party. Holidays offer excellent sources for themes—Bastille Day, Halloween, Christmas, for example—and it's fun to think up appropriate foods and decorations.